D0771003

# IRELAND

## GALLERY BOOKS
An Imprint of W. H. Smith Publishers Inc.
112 Madison Avenue
New York City 10016

This edition first published in U.S.
in 1990 by Gallery Books,
an imprint of W.H. Smith Publishers, Inc.
112 Madison Avenue, New York, New York 10016


ISBN 0-8317-0253-2


Printed and bound in Spain


For rights information about the photographs in
this book please contact:


The Image Bank
111 Fifth Avenue, New York, NY 10003


Producer: Solomon M. Skolnick
Writer: Coleen O'Shea
Design Concept: Lesley Ehlers
Designer: Ann-Louise Lipman
Editor: Joan E. Ratajack
Production: Valerie Zars
Photo Researcher: Edward Douglas
Assistant Photo Researcher: Robert V. Hale
Editorial Assistant: Carol Raguso

*Title page:* This fine Celtic cross in
County Mayo is an excellent example of
a carved standing stone. *Opposite:* This
brilliantly illuminated portrait of Christ
is found in the eighth-century manu-
script, the Book of Kells, housed at
Trinity College, Dublin.

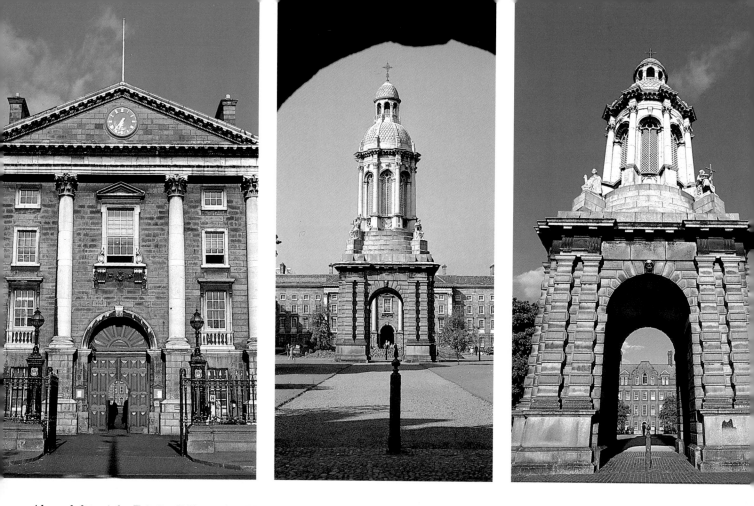

*Above, left to right:* Trinity College, the oldest university in Ireland (it was founded by Elizabeth I of England), is today a world-famous center of learning. *Below:* A statue of George Salmon, provost of the college from 1888 to 1904, stands before the Trinity College Memorial Building.

I reland is a magical island, where lore, legends, and limericks color the landscape. From the velvet green countryside in the mid-country to the high, dark cliffs that meet the cold North Atlantic to the brilliant purple moorlands and the bleak, desolate bogs, Ireland is a land where the mists rise to reveal a place of breathtaking beauty.

The Emerald Isle, known for the many rich shades of green that carpet the earth, is only 300 miles long and about half as wide, yet within this relatively small area is a landscape that changes with every bend in the road. The conventional image of Ireland is that of thatch-roofed and whitewashed cottages bordered by stone walls and scented hedgerows, giving way to lush rolling hills where sheep graze. Though there are many such sights, the great physical attractions of Ireland are splendidly varied. Few places can match the rugged beauty of Connemara and the Aran Islands in the west, the splendor of the wild Dingle Peninsula, the extraordinary towering pillars of the Giant's Causeway, the majestic drama of the Cliffs

*This page, top to bottom:* A splendid example of eighteenth-century architecture, the imposing Parliament House in College Green is now the Bank of Ireland building. It originally housed the Irish Parliament during the period of Home Rule. The National Gallery, whose collection includes works by Rembrandt, Monet, and Cézanne, was designed by Francis Fowke and opened in 1864.

of Moher, or the spectacular scenery of the Ring of Kerry on the Iveragh Peninsula.

Ireland today is composed of two political entities on the second largest island of what was once known as the British Isles. It is divided between the Irish Republic, an independent nation of 26 counties and covering 27,000 square miles, with a population of about 3.5 million, and Northern Ireland, in the northernmost part of the island. Northern Ireland, a province of the United Kingdom, has an estimated population of about 1.5 million and is made up of six counties that cover about 5,400 square miles. Although the political climate of the two Irelands is widely different, they share a rich and textured history and a people who are graced with a glorious natural charm. The island is in the North Atlantic, separated from England by the Irish Sea, from Wales by St. George's Channel, and from Scotland, its nearest neighbor, by the North Channel. The weather is moist but mild, as Ireland is blessed with warm currents from the Gulf Stream. In fact, palm trees are an unexpected sight on this northern, temperate isle.

*This page:* Located near St. Stephen's Green and the National Museum, Grafton Street is Dublin's most fashionable shopping district. *Opposite:* At night, dramatic lighting colors O'Connell Street, an extension of the O'Connell Bridge.

A statue of Sir John Gay, author of *The Beggar's Opera*, is one of several statues on O'Connell Street. *Below:* Humorously nicknamed "Floozie in a Jacuzzi," this statue on O'Connell Street entertains passersby.

The heart and capital of Eire, as the republic is known, is Dublin. The classical beauty of this 1,000-year-old city is an inspiration. Its well-tended parks, splendid Georgian squares, and ancient monuments are just some of the many attractions. Joyce, Yeats, Shaw, and Wilde are just a few of the literary giants who have walked its streets. Several of these luminaries came to the city to attend Trinity College, the oldest university in Ireland.

Dublin is a friendly city where traditional music is often heard spilling from the pubs, many of which are located in the shadows of the imposing façades of St. Patrick's and Christchurch cathedrals. To the south rise the Dublin hills and the Wicklow Mountains, and the river Liffey makes its way to the sea through the city. Dublin became a major center for European trade early in its history because of both the river and the city's location on the curve of Dublin Bay.

The Green Isle's history is long, and the landscape is strewn with remarkable evidence of the past. Cairns and forts, standing stones or dolmens, abbeys, high crosses, monasteries, and feudal castles

*Above:* A masterpiece of architecture, the Custom House was designed by Dublin's greatest architect, James Gandon. It was completed in 1791, and is surmounted by a graceful copper dome and a statue of Hope. *Right:* On the steps of the General Post Office, which was built in 1818, Padraic Pearse declared in 1916 that Ireland would forevermore be an independent republic.

*Preceding page:* Guinness, the popular black beer, has been brewed in Dublin since 1759. *Below:* A boat rests at dockside in Dublin Bay.

The river Liffey, shown here at the center of the business district, winds its way through Dublin and is spanned by 11 bridges.

The Halfpenny Bridge, named for its original toll, crosses the river Liffey and is a popular pedestrian walkway.

trace the progression of humanity through time.

Archaeological excavation reveals that Ireland was visited first by hunters and fishermen from Scotland in roughly 6,000 B.C., but cultivation of the land did not begin until some 3,000 years later. Settlements were then established by farmers who used stone tools, and since those ancient times there has been a continuous agricultural tradition.

Built in 1729, Parliament House was the first of an impressive series of public buildings erected in Dublin during the eighteenth century. *Below:* Imposing columns front the entrance of Dublin's City Hall.

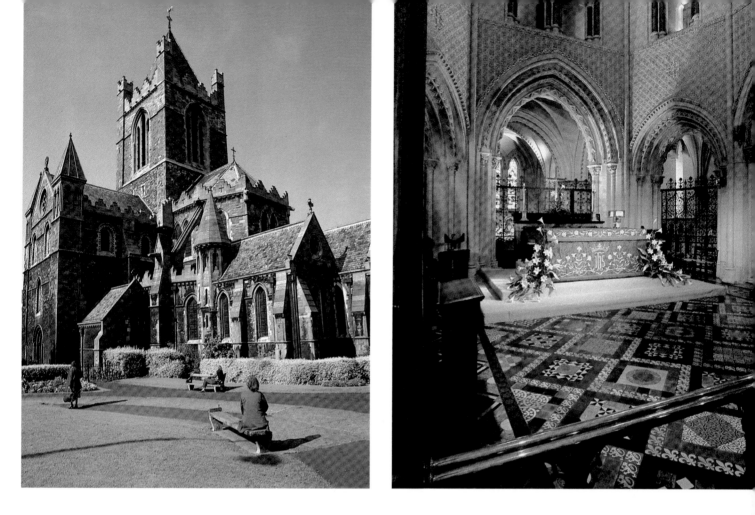

*This page:* Christchurch Cathedral was founded in 1038 and erected on the site of the ancient city. Much restored over the ages, this now-Protestant cathedral was the scene of many important events in Ireland's history.

*Above:* Completed on the north bank of the river Liffey in 1802, the Four Courts building is resplendent with its domes. *Below, left:* Dublin Castle was for 400 years the seat of English rule. *Right:* St. Patrick's Cathedral houses the grave of Jonathan Swift, author of *Gulliver's Travels* and dean of the cathedral from 1713 to 1745.

SUNLIGHT CHAMBERS

Traces of the early settlers are abundant. Court cairns, underground tombs made of long chambers divided into compartments, survive to this day. The most impressive of these is the earthen mound at the Newgrange Neolithic Burial Tomb in the Boyne Valley in County Meath, an extraordinary ancient tomb on an impressive site that predates the pyramids. Perhaps

*Above:* This lovely fresco decorates the facade of a building once used as a soap factory. *Right:* George Bernard Shaw, author of *Man and Superman* and *Pygmalion,* is a favorite son of Dublin, born there in 1854.

even more well known are the mythic standing circles that are sprinkled throughout the country. They were constructed during the Bronze Age, about the time the Celts arrived in Ireland.

It is not clear when the first Celts arrived from Europe, but certainly by the end of the fifth century B.C. Ireland was entirely populated by Celts who displaced the Stone Age settlers. The Celtic tribes, descended from a group of Indo-European warriors, were linked by a common language root and religion, and by a fractious temperament that encouraged fierce battles between the clans.

Today, Ireland owes an enormous debt to the Celts, who later were called the Gaels. The Irish language, Gaelic, is the official language of the country, although English is spoken by an overwhelming majority. Safeguards to protect the Irish vernacular came from government grants to regions where lilting, ancient Irish is in everyday use. Called *Gaeltachts,* "Gaelic-speaking areas" and primarily located along the western seaboard, these remote, scenic regions are popular tourist stops. The largest of these *Gaeltachts* are in counties Donegal, Galway, Mayo, and, in County Kerry, the delightful Dingle Peninsula. The peninsula stretches some 30 miles

*This page:* Picturesque bars, shops, and city folk color the streets of Dublin.

*Above, left to right:* Neatly tended windowboxes decorate this quintessentially Georgian facade. M. J. O'Neill's is one of the many warm and friendly pubs that dot Dublin's streets. Highlighted with red and gold, the Long Race pub is a favorite Dublin gathering place. *Below:* A soothing "cuppa" tea welcomes customers to this charming spot.

*Preceding page:* Lusk Round Tower and the nearby churchyard contain some fine medieval tombs. This sixth-century monument is in the handsome fishing village of Rush, County Dublin. *This page, above:* Mellifont Abbey, County Louth, now in ruins, was built in 1142 by the first Cistercians to come to Ireland. *Right:* The Cross of Muireadach in Monasterboice, a fifth-century monastic settlement, was made in the early tenth century and is considered by many to be the most perfect High Cross. Just about its entire surface is carved with scenes from the Bible, the only way the illiterate could "read" the holy scriptures.

*Above:* The Boyne Valley of County Meath comprises over 40 related prehistoric sites, the most important of which are the passage graves at Dowth, Knowth, and Newgrange.
*Left:* Newgrange in County Meath, an extraordinary relic of the Neolithic age (c. 3700–2000 B.C.), is a huge repository of the dead. *Opposite:* Nestled in the picturesque Wicklow Mountains is Glendalough, Ireland's most important early Christian monastic settlement. It was founded in the sixth century by St. Kevin, a hermit.

These church ruins stand near Hook Head, County Waterford, where a 700-year-old lighthouse guides sailors home. *Below:* Birdwatchers delight in the variety of fowl to be seen on the Saltee Islands, Ireland's largest bird sanctuary.

west of Tralee and has more intriguing antiquities, historic sites, and varied mountain scenery than any other part of Ireland.

The Celts warred endlessly among themselves, laid the foundation for the geographic division of the land among the clans, elected kings and chieftains, and contributed the rich culture of the learned people known as Druids. The Druids, famous in lore and literature, provided the mystic flavor to the Irish people. Although little but legend remains from this distant past, it is known that the Hill of Tara, near Naven in County Meath, was the home of the ancient Celtic kings. For more than 2,000 years it played a significant role in Ireland's Celtic culture. During the early Christian era, the Roman Empire stretched its reach across most of Western Europe, yet Ireland was one of the few areas to escape its domination. There are not many records from this time, but it is clear the people began to convert to Christianity when Saint Patrick, a native of England, arrived from Rome in roughly A.D. 432. Tradition claims that Patrick used the shamrock to illustrate the doctrine of the Trinity and his staff to drive the snakes from the land.

*This page, top to bottom:* This working, thatch-roofed windmill, built in 1846 in County Wexford, is a monument to Ireland's agricultural heritage. Attractive thatch-roofed cottages grace Kilmore Quay, a fishing village in Wexford County. Fishing boats cluster in Kilmore Quay.

Saint Patrick visited Cashel, the seat of ancient chieftains, in about A.D. 450 to baptize King Aenghus. *Below:* Daylight floods the strikingly beautiful ruins at Cashel.

At about this time, the great monastic cities began to develop as religious baronies and universities, nourishing the intellectual life of the land. Among the settlements that flowered during the early Middle Ages was Glendalough in County Wicklow, founded by Saint Kevin in the sixth century. The ruins here are particularly handsome, the setting picturesque. The Rock of Cashel, which dominates the Tipperary countryside, offers one of the most spectacular panoramas of the country and also presents fascinating monastic ruins.

Saint Patrick was so successful in converting the islanders to Christianity that Irish monks traveled abroad to spread the gospel. Irish art and the monastic life emerged as the most important civilizing factors of the early Middle Ages both in Ireland and abroad. One brilliant example of Irish art is the magnificently illuminated Book of Kells, an illustrated book of the Gospels, now the most precious volume in Dublin's Trinity College. The Derrynaflan Chalice, also housed at Trinity College, is another treasure.

*This page, top to bottom:* Offering some of the most magnificent vistas in Ireland, the Rock of Cashel, County Tipperary, is a popular tourist spot. Lichens grow on the interior walls of one of the structures at Cashel, now a national monument. Once the seat of kings and medieval bishops, the Rock of Cashel rises above the green plains and dominates the Tipperary landscape.

*This page:* Waterford crystal epitomizes Irish handcrafted products. The largest crystal factory in the world, Waterford employs more than 3,000 people. Visitors can watch the manufacturing process from mouth blowing to hand cutting.

The Vikings were next to arrive on the Irish shore, invading in 795. The warlike Gaels were no match for the predatory Danes who raided along the coast, destroying monasteries and their treasured libraries. The maurauding Norse pirates built garrisons along the eastern seaboard, claiming kingships and establishing Ireland's first cities and ports at the sites of conquered settlements. These bases for inland marches of conquest evolved into the cities of Dublin, Limerick, Cork, and Waterford.

Beginning in 1169, a succession of Anglo-Norman and Norman-Welsh knight-adventurers came to Ireland. These brilliant and sophisticated soldiers claimed control and brought to pass the most important event in the island's history: Ireland became a colony of the British Crown. The Normans and Gaels shared skills and intermarried. The Normans became, so the saying goes, more "Irish than the Irish themselves." When this integration occurred, Britain looked on with displeasure and eventually instituted strict measures in the form of the Statutes of Kilkenny to keep Gaelic influence from spreading further.

*This page:* Meticulous care is taken by artisans who work on delicate porcelain figurines at the Irish Dresden factory, which moved to County Limerick from Volkstedt, Germany, 25 years ago.

At Dysert O'Dea, County Clare, a Romanesque portal demonstrates the skill of early stone carvers, who sculpted intricate human and animal heads.

The graceful Gothic spires of St. Finbar's Cathedral, built between 1867 and 1879, dominate the skyline in Cork. *Below:* Nineteenth-century storefronts are well tended in Cork, a city known for its friendliness and warmth. *Overleaf:* Verdant fields and pasturelands slope to the sea on the Beara Peninsula in West Cork.

The turrets of Black Rock Castle gleam in the brilliant sunlight. *Below:* Not far from the city of Cork is the legendary Blarney Stone.

Fierce uprisings against the statutes and against British rule began in 1366 and climaxed during the Reformation. Oliver Cromwell, England's Lord Protector, landed in Ireland in 1649, and brutally crushed the Gaelic population.

The Ascendancy followed. This involved British Anglo-Protestants who went to the Catholic island colony to claim land confiscated from the Irish as reward for service. These British landed gentry became a new, privileged class determined to preserve their special rights through loyalty to the British Crown. Today, the Irish landscape is dappled with magnificent castles such as the splendid Lismore Castle in County Waterford, the Irish home of the Duke of Devonshire; Tallyrally Castle and Gardens, the home of the earls of Landford since the seventeenth century; Castlepollard in County Westmeath; and a great many others. Several castles have now been converted to first-class hotels.

These new British landowners sternly imposed their own culture, laws, and Protestant religion, while tariffs strangled the island's economy. Reduced to serfdom in their native land, the Irish masses again threatened insurgency, but the English government quelled the uprisings.

In 1847, the potato, the staple food of the common people, succumbed to blight for the second time, and the Great Famine descended over Ireland. This terrible catastrophe decimated the population; over 1 million people died and another million fled.

The British did not step in to rescue this impoverished land. Rather, foodstuffs from Ireland that were not affected by the blight and which could have fed the starving were exported to England to pay rents to absentee landowners.

Centuries of often violent strife tainted the relationship between England and Ireland. Hopes of equality were repeatedly dashed, but the brutal Easter Rebellion of 1916 finally opened the door for the beginnings of a kind of truce. In 1949 the Republic of Eire declared its independence from England while Northern Ireland pursued its relationship within the Commonwealth, though civil disobedience and guerilla war still erupt. Today, it is hoped that peace will soon visit the land.

For a land that carries such a checkered past and present, the friendliness and warmth of the native people are legendary.

*This page, top to bottom:* Hoping to be blessed with the "gift of gab," a tourist kisses the fabled Blarney Stone, set high in the castle walls. The quaint and well-preserved seaside village of Kinsale, County Cork, is the site of the renowned Gourmet Festival. A favorite of Irish and European yachting enthusiasts, Kinsale is one of the most scenic ports in Ireland.

The distinctive whitewashed cottages and stone walls of the Dingle Peninsula add beauty to a dramatic coastline. *Below:* Blasket Island, Dingle, a sparsely populated island in the southwest, is home to these ruins.

*Above, left to right:* The fifth-century Reask Stone in Kerry is an example of a grave slab carved with early Christian symbols. The Oratory of Gallarus, a relic of early Christianity, is so watertight that it has stayed dry inside for a thousand years. The wild landscape of Dingle Peninsula is dotted with *clocháns,* dwellings built of stones fitted together without mortar. *Below:* These beehive-shaped ruins were a sixth-century monastic settlement on Skellig Michael.

*This page:* A quiet village divided by the Sneen River, Sneen is a pleasant stop on the Ring of Kerry, a popular scenic drive.

*This page:* Distinctive stone walls edge farmland along the Ring of Kerry. *Overleaf:* A splendid touring road, Connor (or Conair) Pass winds through the central Dingle mountains and offers stunning views.

*Preceding page:* Impressive in its simplicity, this standing arch gives way to a splendid panorama. *This page:* Bunratty Castle, a fine tower house dating from 1460, is at least the fourth structure to have been erected on this spot near the bank of the river Ratty.

*Preceding page:* Ennis Abbey, County Clare, once a fine educational institution boasting over 350 friars and 600 students, is known for its many decorated tombs and gravestones. *This page:* Known as a dolmen (derived from a Breton word meaning "stone table"), the Gleninsheen Wedge Tomb (c. 2000 B.C.) is located in the Burren, County Clare. *Below:* Sheep placidly graze by the sea in Glencolumbkille, County Donegal.

In Ireland, they say, there are no strangers, only friends you have yet to meet. Emerging from a great oral tradition, the Irish have elevated conversation to an art form. Indeed, Blarney Castle in County Cork is the home of the legendary Blarney Stone. Tradition has it that whoever kisses it will be blessed with the gift of eloquence. Clearly the Irish take their reputation to heart: The pace of life on the isle is such that there is always time for a chat on a country road, a heartfelt invitation for a "cuppa" at home, or a "jar" of Guinness at the local pub.

The Irish pub has a world-famous reputation. That should come as no surprise, for Ireland has 10,500 pubs in the republic and another 2,000 in the north. Pub crawling is a national pastime. Some are modern ones that serve elegant food and drink; others are age darkened and rich with history. Conversation, music, and beer flow. Brewed for the first time in Dublin in 1759, the robust black brew known as Guinness stout has many devotees worldwide. Today the Guinness Brewery in Dublin is the largest exporting stout brewery in the world. But stout isn't the

*Preceding pages:* The great, plunging Cliffs of Moher create one of the most dramatic coastlines in all of Europe. *This page, top to bottom:* Ancient standing stones reflect the setting sun on Machric Moor in the Aran Islands, a group of three islands 30 miles from the mouth of Galway Bay. A *curragh,* a traditional fishing craft, is carried away from the tides in the Aran Islands. Stone walls criss-cross Inishmore, the largest of the islands.

neatly stacked pile of peat awaits winter, when it will be burned to keep the chill from the corners of this cottage. *Below:* With a view of he Twelve Bens in the background, these Connemara peat bogs offer a uniquely Irish sight and scent.

Carefully constructed haystacks dot this lush emerald field in County Galway. *Below:* Mules are still the most common means of transportation in the wilds of Connemara.

only local beverage. Whiskey is traditional, too. The word itself derives from the Irish *uisge beatha,* meaning "water of life." The top brands are Jameson, Bushmills, Power, and Paddy. The fiery, white, distilled spirit known as *poitin* (also known as *poteen*), is highly alcoholic and frequently toxic. It is illegal, but bootlegging does continue the tradition of a more dangerous past.

Another favorite pastime in Ireland involves the festivals that take place throughout the year. These cover a wide range of interests. Among the highlights are the Galway Oyster Festival, the Rose of Tralee pageant, the Dublin Horse Show, the Yeats Summer School, and the Dublin Theatre Festival. Although literature and acting both have a noble past, a successful contemporary theatrical tradition flowers in Ireland as well, perhaps due to the hearty roots of the oral Gaelic tradition.

For the sports minded, there's horse racing throughout the year, with the biggest event being the Budweiser Irish Derby in Kildare, County Kildare. Irish horse gatherings are remarkable events that range from visiting the celebrated stud farms (which enjoy tax-free status) to hunting, jumping, and of course, racing. Steeplechasing, born in Ireland in

*Above:* A mare and her foal graze by the coast in the west mountains of Connemara. *Right:* A bicycle rests against a picket fence surrounding a typical whitewashed house in County Galway.

Topped by traditional thatching, this cottage near Ballyconeeley fronts the rugged Atlantic coastline. *Below:* Great care is lavished on the hedges and flowerbeds surrounding this Connemara cottage.

Looking like something out of a fairytale, this castle is in County Galway.

*Preceding page:* Clonfert Cathedral in County Galway, south of Ballinasloe, is a splendid example of Irish Romanesque architecture. *This page, above:* A marker commemorates the visit of John Fitzgerald Kennedy, 34th president of the United States, to County Galway. *Below:* Of particular interest to American tourists are these tombstones of Kennedy's forebears.

The smiling faces of children greet visitors to this Irish village. *Below:* A rural bank on wheels passes a donkey on an idyllic Connemara road.

William Butler Yeats, the poet who so loved this part of the country, is buried at Drumcliffe within sight of Benbulben, one of Ireland's most dramatic mountains. *Below:* One can easily imagine townspeople gathering around the market cross in Cong, County Mayo, throughout the ages.

1752, is one of the most exciting events to watch. Only the brave join in this wild race over the countryside. Otherwise, it is easy to mingle with owners, breeders, trainers, and riders at any one or more of the over 300 horse events held nationwide annually.

For other sports enthusiasts, there are the great sports of Gaelic football, hurling, and certainly, golf, with extraordinary courses at Ballybunion, County Kerry; Portmarnock, County Dublin; and Killarney, County Killarney, to name only three of the more than 200 courses that dot the countryside.

While waterholes may be the nemesis of stalwart golfers, for the angler, Ireland is paradise. This water-dappled kingdom of 32,000 square miles contains 9,000 miles of river, including the beloved Shannon River, and over 600,000 acres of lakes (or *loughs*). Almost all this water holds fish, and the wild brown trout are considered the best in Europe. Angling is an important tourist activity in the Irish Republic. Eager "reelers" await the yearly return of salmon and sea trout to freshwater.

Haystacks like these are a typical sight in Donegal. *Below:* Puckish charm glimmers in the friendly smile of a Blasket Islander.

Sparkling crystal, china, and glassware are just a few of Ireland's internationally known products. Manufactured mainly in counties Waterford, Galway, and Caven, elegant stemware is one of Ireland's most famous exports. One happy result of the Industrial Revolution's bypassing Ireland is that the legacy of these lovely handicrafts remains. Whether it is for heavy lead crystal from prestigious Waterford, fine lace, authentic Irish linen, or the superlative tweeds, plaids, and knits, shopping in Ireland is a delight and any of these items can become a treasured family heirloom.

From natural scenery that is endlessly captivating to monastic sites and holy places, from remarkable castles, houses, and dramatic gardens to traditional crafts, Ireland is an ancient land with the promise of an exciting tomorrow. The magic of history, mists, and stone mingle to create the splendid heritage that may be traced through its architecture. And as these structures, both primitive and majestic, standing or in ruins, seem to rise in the mists at dawn, it is easy to believe that faeries and leprechauns roam this treasured isle.

This picture-perfect castle and its exquisite gardens in Glenveagh are part of a national park that is home to deer and peregrine falcons. *Overleaf:* Caribbean-blue water washes the Atlantic shoreline in northern Donegal County.

# Index of Photography

TIB indicates The Image Bank